CODE RED

MAY 6, 1937

The Hindenburg Disaster

by Aaron Feigenbaum

Consultant: Paul F. Johnston,
Washington, D.C.

BEARPORT
PUBLISHING

New York, New York

Credits

Cover and Title Page, © The Granger Collection, New York; 3, © The Granger Collection, New York; 4-5, © CORBIS; 6, © Mary Evans Picture Library/Alamy; 7, © AP Images; 9, © Hulton Archive/Getty Images/Newscom.com; 10, © CORBIS; 11, © Brown Brothers; 12, © Scherl/SV-Bilderdienst; 13, © Bettmann/Corbis; 14-15, © Arthur Cofod/Pictures Inc./Time Life Pictures/Getty Images; 16, © POPPERFOTO/Alamy; 17, © Bettmann/Corbis; 18, © Bettmann/Corbis; 19, © Mansell/Time Life Pictures/Getty Images; 20, © Bettmann/Corbis; 21, © Bettmann/Corbis; 22, © American Stock/Getty Images/Newscom.com; 23, © AP Images; 24, © Zuma Press/Newscom.com; 25, © Bettmann/Corbis; 26T, © Max Frei; 26B, © Karl R. Martin/Shutterstock; 27, © Max Frei; 28T, © STAFF/AFP/Getty Images; 28B, © U.S. Naval Historical Center; 29T, © ullstein bild / The Granger Collection, New York; 29B, © AP Images; 29 Background, Clipart.com; 30, © The Granger Collection, New York; 31, © American Stock/Getty Images/Newscom.com.

Publisher: Kenn Goin
Project Editor: Lisa Wiseman
Creative Director: Spencer Brinker
Photo Researcher: Marty Levick
Design: Dawn Beard Creative

Library of Congress Cataloging-in-Publication Data

Feigenbaum, Aaron.
  The Hindenburg disaster / by Aaron Feigenbaum.
    p. cm. — (Code red)
  Includes bibliographical references and index.
  ISBN-13: 978-1-59716-361-3 (library binding)
  ISBN-10: 1-59716-361-9 (library binding)
  1. Hindenburg (Airship) —Juvenile literature. 2. Aircraft accidents—New
Jersey—Juvenile literature. 3. Airships—Germany—Juvenile literature. I. Title.

  TL659.H5F45 2007
  363.12'465—dc22
                                                    2006026672

For more information, write to Bearport Publishing Company, Inc., 101 Fifth Avenue, Suite 6R, New York, New York 10003. Printed in the United States of America.

10 9 8 7 6 5 4 3 2 1

Contents

A Day Unlike Any Other

On the evening of May 6, 1937, passengers on the **airship** *Hindenburg* were getting ready to land. The weather was clearing over the **air station** at Lakehurst, New Jersey. Captain Max Pruss had just announced that they would soon be on the ground.

Five hundred feet (152 m) below, a crowd of people waited to greet the passengers. The travelers had flown all the way from Germany. Newspaper reporters scribbled notes. Photographers pointed their cameras to the sky and snapped pictures. The landing of the world's largest airship was big news! People did not know they were about to witness a terrible tragedy.

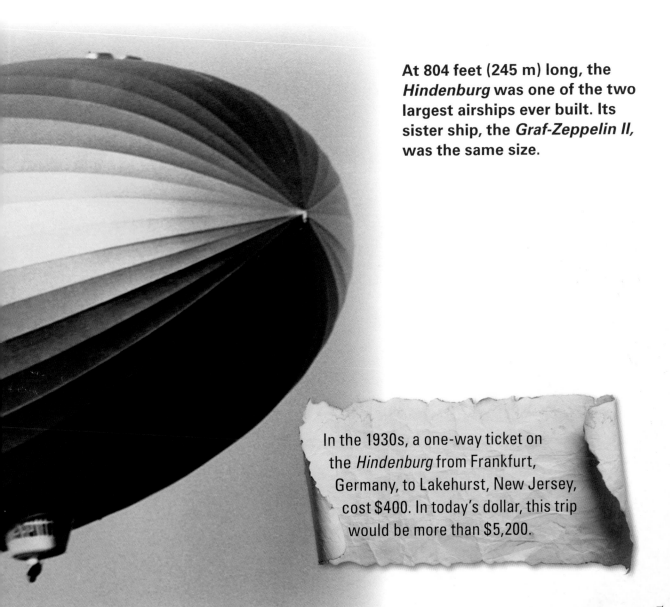

At 804 feet (245 m) long, the *Hindenburg* was one of the two largest airships ever built. Its sister ship, the *Graf-Zeppelin II,* was the same size.

In the 1930s, a one-way ticket on the *Hindenburg* from Frankfurt, Germany, to Lakehurst, New Jersey, cost $400. In today's dollar, this trip would be more than $5,200.

Why Airships Can Fly

The *Hindenburg* was not the first airship used for passenger travel. On July 2, 1900, Ferdinand von Zeppelin flew five people on the *LZ-1*.

Zeppelin understood that airships could fly because they are filled with gases that are lighter than air. Most airships use **helium**. The *Hindenburg*, however, was filled with an even lighter gas called **hydrogen**.

The first passenger airship, the *LZ-1*, floats over Lake Constance, Germany.

Airships are sometimes called zeppelins in honor of the man who invented them, Ferdinand von Zeppelin.

The Zeppelin Company began building the *Hindenburg* in 1931. It was so big that it took five years to complete. Finally, on May 6, 1936, the *Hindenburg* lifted off the ground in Germany. It was making its first trip to America.

A hangar is a storage place for aircraft. A special one was built for the *Hindenburg*. This airship was too big to fit in a regular airport hangar.

"If you want to travel in a beautiful way your first choice has to be a zeppelin."

—Eugen Bentele, *Hindenburg* mechanic

7

A Job at the Top of the World

Fourteen-year-old Werner Franz worked as a **cabin boy** on the *Hindenburg*. He loved his job, but on May 6, 1937, he was disappointed. He had hoped to go to a movie in New York City once the great airship landed. Bad weather, however, had made the *Hindenburg* late. Werner probably wouldn't be able to get to a show in time.

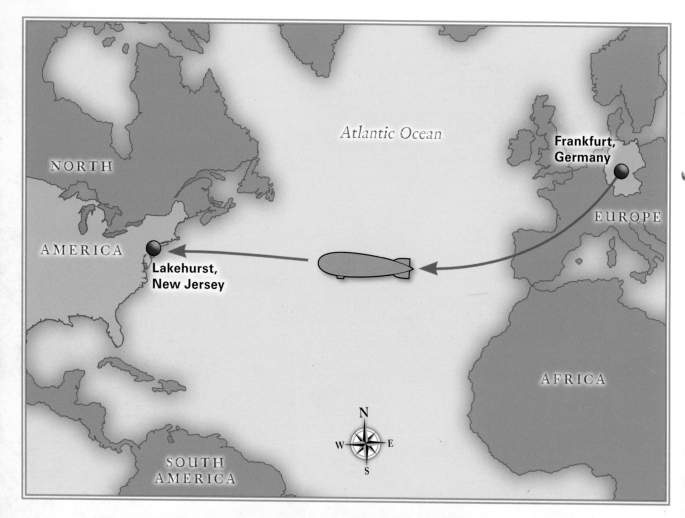

The *Hindenburg* took two and a half days to fly from Frankfurt, Germany, to Lakehurst, New Jersey. Today, an airplane can make the same trip in just six hours.

Werner was also upset that he couldn't join the other crew members in the ship's **bow**. He loved looking out the bow's large windows as the ship landed. Unfortunately, he had too many chores to finish in the kitchen.

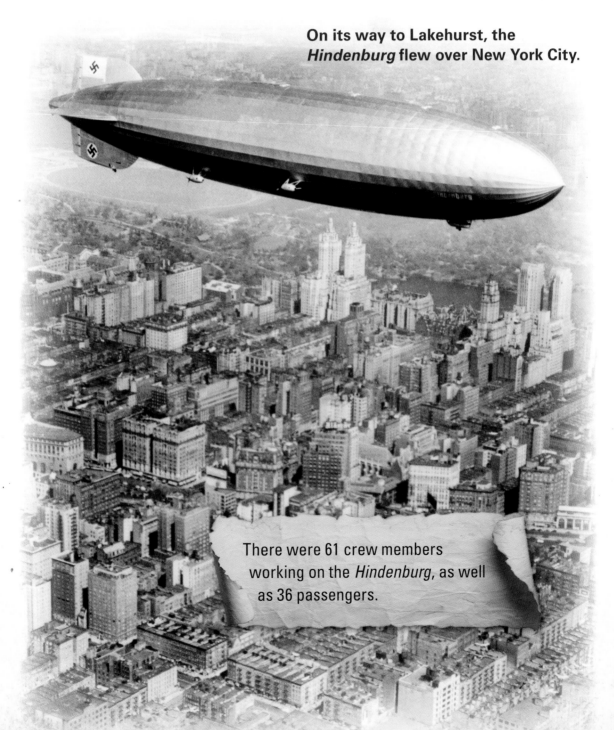

On its way to Lakehurst, the *Hindenburg* flew over New York City.

There were 61 crew members working on the *Hindenburg*, as well as 36 passengers.

A Floating Hotel

The *Hindenburg* made its way to the landing area. Radio announcer Herbert Morrison looked up from where he was standing on the ground. He was amazed at how big the airship looked.

Like a cruise ship, the *Hindenburg* had rooms with beds and a sink.

Inside, the *Hindenburg* was very **luxurious**. Some people called it a "floating hotel." Passengers slept in comfortable **cabins**. There was a dining room that served fancy meals. The airship also had a lounge where passengers could play cards.

In the reading and writing room, passengers could write letters using special *Hindenburg* stationery.

On most flights, passengers could play an **aluminum** piano. However, the piano wasn't on board during the May 1937 trip.

Something's Gone Wrong

At 7:25 P.M. the *Hindenburg* **hovered** just 200 feet (61 m) above the airfield. The **ground crew** rushed to grab the dangling ropes dropped from the ship.

It usually took many men to move the *Hindenburg* at the beginning and end of its flights. On May 6, 1937, however, the airship caught fire before the ground crew was able to grab the ropes.

The *Hindenburg* was named after the former German president, Paul von Hindenburg.

Meanwhile, Helmut Lau was working in the ship's **stern**. He stood under the bags of hydrogen gas that kept the ship afloat.

Suddenly, he heard a strange noise overhead. Looking up, he saw a small flame near the gas containers. Then a jolt went through the rest of the ship. The mighty airship tilted backward and giant flames shot up into the air. The *Hindenburg* was on fire and beginning to fall!

"I heard a big noise and then I saw the flames. The flames were going through the whole ship and then forwards to the bow.**"**
–Captain Max Pruss

Down the Hatch

Alone in the crew's kitchen, Werner felt the *Hindenburg* **lurch** backward. He knew that something had gone terribly wrong. He scrambled out of the kitchen and ran to the **catwalk**. A giant fireball was coming his way! If Werner didn't get out of the *Hindenburg* soon, he would surely die.

Suddenly, a big water tank burst right above him. The water protected him from the fire. Crawling along the catwalk, Werner found a hatch. He kicked it open and jumped. When Werner hit the ground, he ran away from the *Hindenburg* as fast as he could.

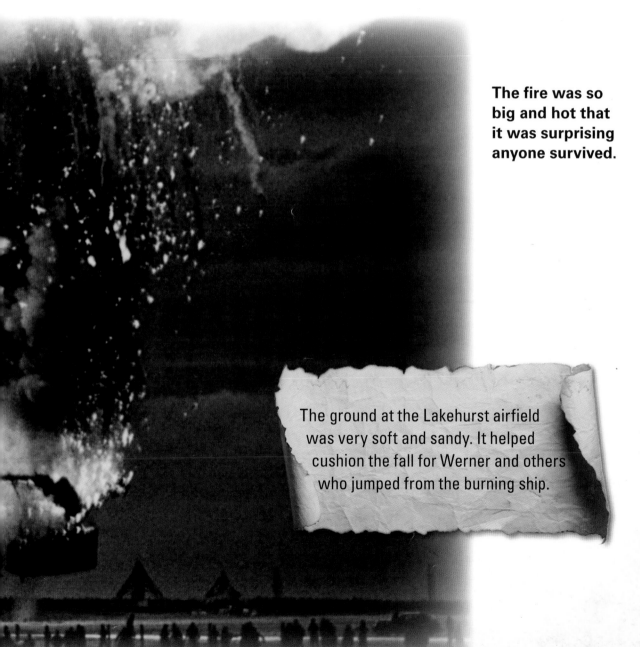

The fire was so big and hot that it was surprising anyone survived.

The ground at the Lakehurst airfield was very soft and sandy. It helped cushion the fall for Werner and others who jumped from the burning ship.

Words Heard Around the World

Reporting from the ground, Herbert Morrison, the radio announcer, couldn't believe what he was seeing. "It burst into flames! . . . it's falling . . ." he yelled into his microphone. "This is one of the worst **catastrophes** in the world! . . . Oh, the **humanity**, and all the passengers screaming around here! Listen, folks, I'm gonna have to stop for a minute because this was the worst thing I've ever witnessed."

The flames leaped hundreds of feet (meters) in the air as the *Hindenburg* struggled to stay afloat.

The *Hindenburg* had never been in an accident before. In 1936, it safely made ten trips to the United States.

Morrison's words were played all around the world the next day. When people listened to his report, they felt as if they were actually watching the disaster. His emotional broadcast became famous.

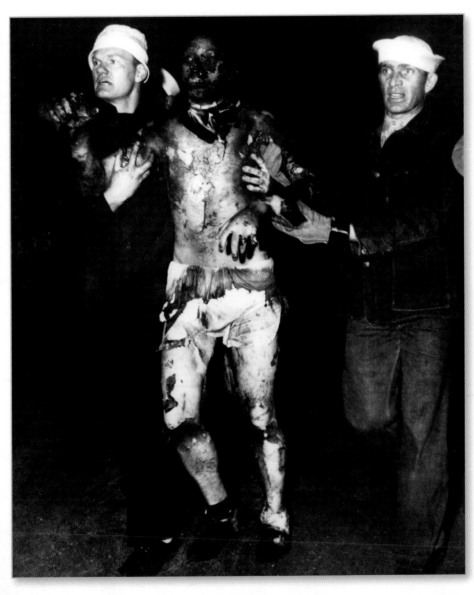

Some of the passengers were able to jump out of the airship before it hit the ground. The American ground crew helped save some of them.

❝ It's lightning, jump! ❞
—Ernst Lehmann, crew member, thinking the airship had been struck by lightning

The Crash

The *Hindenburg* did not crash to the ground all at once. While Werner was trying to escape at the bow, the stern landed on its tail. It stood right next to the base of the **mooring mast**.

The *Hindenburg* on its stern next to the mooring mast

The *Hindenburg*'s top speed was about 85 miles per hour (137 kph).

Seconds later, as Werner ran from the *Hindenburg*, the rest of the ship hit the ground behind him. Burning parts of the ship flew all over the place. Many passengers and crew members were so badly burned that they could hardly walk.

The *Hindenburg* just as it hit the ground

The Great Fire

Everywhere, people were screaming. Flames from the burning ship shot up 200 feet (61 m) into the air. Brave firefighters, who had been standing by in case of an emergency, shouted to one another as they battled the blaze. They, along with the ground crew, rushed toward the burning shell of the ship. They carried the injured people to safety as ambulances rushed to the scene.

As the flames died down, rescue workers began to search for survivors.

After the fire broke out, it took about 32 seconds for the *Hindenburg* to crash.

Sadly, many who survived the crash were so badly injured that they soon died. In total, 36 people died—13 passengers, 22 crewmen, and 1 member of the ground crew.

Those who were strong enough to walk away from the crash tried to help the others to safety.

"It was like a dream, our bodies had no weight. They floated like stars through space."

—Leonhard Adelt, a passenger describing running from the burning *Hindenburg*

What Happened?

Everyone wanted to know why the *Hindenburg* caught fire. Both the German and American governments investigated the crash. They said that a spark **ignited** the ship's hydrogen gas. However, no one knew what had caused the spark.

The *Hindenburg* crash was the biggest news of the day. The number of deaths reported here does not include the member of the ground crew who was also killed.

A German girl named Irene Doehner was the youngest person killed in the *Hindenburg* disaster. She was only 16 years old.

Some scientists think the fire was fueled by the paint on the ship's cover. This special paint was used to make the cover stronger. It was made from some of the same material used to power rockets. To this day, the exact cause of the fire remains a mystery.

The surviving crew members of the *Hindenburg* posed for a picture the day after the crash.

❝ The *Hindenburg* was literally painted with rocket fuel. ❞

–Addison Bain, a scientist who thinks the paint on the *Hindenburg*'s cover fueled the fire

Troubled Times

Many people felt the fire would never have happened if the *Hindenburg* had been powered by helium instead of hydrogen. Helium doesn't burn, while hydrogen catches fire very easily. However, Germany didn't have any of the non-burning gas.

"Helium . . . is the safest thing for air."
–Captain Max Pruss in an interview about the crash in 1960

An aerial view of Berlin, Germany's Olympic Stadium in 1936, taken from inside the *Hindenburg*

At the time, the United States had a large supply of helium. The U.S. government, though, refused to sell it to the Germans. The United States didn't agree with the ideas of the German leader, Adolf Hitler. He often used the *Hindenburg* for **propaganda** purposes. For example, he ordered the Zeppelin Company to display **swastikas** on the airship.

The *Hindenburg* flying over a crowd in Germany that included Adolf Hitler

Some crew members believed the *Hindenburg* had been **sabotaged** by people who hated Hitler.

The End of an Era

Even today, people still remember the *Hindenburg* disaster. Every year, on May 6 at 7:25 P.M., the Navy Lakehurst Historical Society holds a **memorial** service to honor those who died.

The memorial at Lakehurst Airfield on May 6, 2006

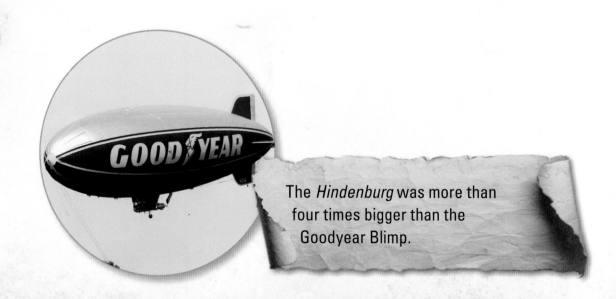

The *Hindenburg* was more than four times bigger than the Goodyear Blimp.

In 2004, 82-year-old Werner Franz traveled from Germany to take part in the service. He also visited a new museum built to help people remember the disaster.

The crash of the *Hindenburg* ended the age of airship travel. It did not, however, keep people out of the sky. The use of airplanes was becoming more common. They were faster and less expensive to fly. Although the *Hindenburg* was gone, the dream of flying still stayed strong.

Werner Franz during his 2004 visit to the Lakehurst Airfield

Many people played an important role in the events connected to the *Hindenburg* disaster. Here are four of them.

Ferdinand von Zeppelin was known as "the father of airships."

- Joined the German Army at age 16
- Traveled to America during the Civil War (1861–1865) and flew in a balloon for the first time while there
- Founded the Zeppelin Company
- Built many airships with his company

Charles Rosendahl was the commanding officer of the Naval Air Station at Lakehurst, New Jersey.

- Learned to fly airships in the 1920s
- Began sailing Navy ships after the *Hindenburg* crashed
- Fought in World War II (1939–1945) and won the Navy Cross, a special award for sailors

Alfred Gröezinger was a cook on the *Hindenburg*.

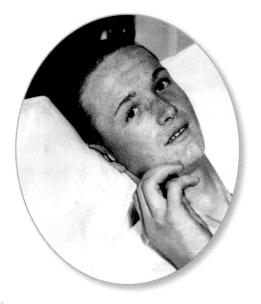

- At age 14, began working for the Zeppelin Company on an airship that flew from Germany to Brazil
- Flew on a total of 142 airship trips
- Helped found a zeppelin museum and often spoke about his experiences on airships

Werner Franz was the cabin boy on the *Hindenburg*.

- Flew on the *Hindenburg* to New York in October 1936
- As a young boy, had hoped to become a captain of an airship when he got older
- Returned to Germany after the crash, where he later married and had a son

Glossary

air station (AIR STAY-shuhn) a place where airships and airplanes can land and park

airship (AIR-*ship*) a large balloon with engines and a passenger compartment attached; the balloon is filled with a gas that is lighter than air to lift the airship off the ground

aluminum (uh-LOO-mi-nuhm) a light-weight, silver-colored metal

bow (BOU) the front end of a ship

cabin boy (KAB-in BOI) a person who performs chores on a ship

cabins (KAB-inz) small, private rooms where passengers and crew can sleep

catastrophes (kuh-TASS-truh-*feez*) sudden disasters

catwalk (KAT-wawk) a narrow bridge or walkway

ground crew (GROUND KROO) a team of mechanics that service aircraft on the ground

helium (HEE-lee-uhm) a very light gas that does not burn

hovered (HUHV-urd) floated in place in the air

humanity (hyoo-MAN-uh-tee) all people; kindness and sympathy

hydrogen (HYE-druh-juhn) a very light gas that catches fire easily

ignited (ig-NITE-id) set on fire or caught fire

lurch (LURCH) to move quickly or suddenly

luxurious (luhk-ZHUH-ree-uhss) fancy and comfortable

memorial (muh-MOR-ee-uhl) something built or done to remember a person or event

mooring mast (MOR-ing MAST) a tower that an airship is tied to, to keep it from floating away

propaganda (*prop*-uh-GAN-duh) often untrue or incomplete information that is spread to gain support for something

sabotaged (SAB-uh-*tahzhd*) destroyed something on purpose

stern (STERN) the rear or back of a ship

swastikas (SWAHSS-tuh-kuhz) ancient symbols adopted by Adolf Hitler and the Nazi party in Germany; usually associated with hatred and anger

Bibliography

Dick, Harold G., and Douglas H. Robinson. *The Golden Age of the Great Passenger Airships:* Graf Zeppelin & Hindenburg. Washington, D.C.: Smithsonian Institution Press (1985).

Heppenheimer, T. A. *A Brief History of Flight: From Balloons to Mach 3 and Beyond.* New York: John Wiley (2000).

www.keepgoing.org/issue20_giant/thirtytwo_seconds.html

www.nlhs.com

Read More

Day, James. *The* Hindenburg *Tragedy.* New York: The Bookwright Press (1989).

Majoor, Mirelle. *Inside the* Hindenburg. Boston: Little, Brown (2000).

O'Brien, Patrick. *The* Hindenburg. New York: Henry Holt (2000).

Tanaka, Shelley. *The Disaster of the* Hindenburg. New York: Scholastic (1993).

Learn More Online

To learn more about the *Hindenburg*, visit
www.bearportpublishing.com/CodeRed

Index

About the Author

Aaron Feigenbaum is an anthropologist, editor, and children's book author. He currently divides his time between the Connecticut coast and the Hawaiian surf.